A Place to Talk

FOR BABIES

Elizabeth Jarman

Featherstone

Published 2013 by Featherstone, an imprint of Bloomsbury Publishing plc
50 Bedford Square, London, WC1B 3DP
www.bloomsbury.com

ISBN 978-1-4081-8681-7

A CIP record for this publication is available from the British Library.

Printed and bound in China by C&C Offset Printing Co Ltd, Shenzhen,
Guangdong

10 9 8 7 6 5 4 3 2 1

This book is produced using paper that is made from wood grown in
managed, sustainable forests. It is natural, renewable and recyclable.
The logging and manufacturing processes conform to the environmental
regulations of the country of origin.

To see our full range of titles
visit www.bloomsbury.com

Contents

Introduction

Caring for babies and supporting their development can be one of the most rewarding but also one of the most demanding jobs. We know that babies are born with natural desire and ability to learn, but they need settings which create the right opportunities for optimum development. Adults working with babies must be highly skilled as they have to rely on interpreting babies' communications and perspectives in order to create spaces which are aligned to their needs, their developmental stage and their many interests within a new, fascinating and sometimes confusing world. Close relationships with carers are fundamental. It is through sensitive relationships that special places can be created and resourced which ensure that babies will thrive and build firm foundations for the future.

A Place to Talk for Babies considers the significant role that the physical environment can play in supporting babies' speaking and listening skills, their emotional well-being and their desire to explore and investigate.

This book includes:
- a summary of some of the key environmental influences, collated from research studies
- lots of examples of ways that practitioners, teachers and parents/carers have offered spaces specifically for babies in different contexts
- questions to prompt action
- sign-posts to further information.

Five environmental factors to consider

Following a review of research and practice in a wide range of contexts we have identified five particularly important environmental points to consider when creating spaces designed to encourage babies' speaking and listening skills. These points are equally important at all stages of a child's education.

1 The physical space needs to set the scene for meaningful interaction and appropriate care to take place.

Establishing a clear understanding of babies' development will inform the way that you plan your learning environment. The way that the physical space is arranged communicates a great deal to babies about what is possible there and hugely affects the way that they feel.

2 Practitioners should make the most of the space available, both inside and out.

It's important to view learning spaces as a whole, including both inside and out and make the most of what's available. Across the area, babies need a variety of spaces, but particularly softer spaces to provide comfort and security and other spaces which support physical development and movement. It is important to remember that the adult caring for babies needs to be comfortable too in order to offer sensitive support to each baby.

3 Spaces should take account of physical factors (e.g. noise, colour and light) that can impact on how babies respond.

Noise
Noises in the environment can sometimes be very frightening and overwhelming for babies. A noisy environment makes listening difficult and confusing which will have a negative effect on the development of listening and speaking skills needed for effective language development.

Colour
Colours need to be chosen carefully as it can affect how babies feel and respond. Overly colourful environments can be too stimulating for babies and can make them unsettled or distressed. A calmer environment will support a baby's ability to focus and interact.

Light

Current research confirms that we are all energised by natural sunlight and that children learn faster in spaces with natural light. Babies are no exception to this! Babies are very sensitive to the bright lighting so often used in settings, so lighting should be modified to create a gentler and more homely environment.

4 The environment should not be overly busy but should provoke interest and exploration.

Too many choices for babies can be very confusing and can make the whole environment feel overpowering. Storage options should therefore be carefully considered and the quantity and type of resources should be developmentally appropriate. Sensory stimulation is vital for babies' brain development. The use of natural and everyday resources can particularly support this.

5 Spaces should be viewed from the babies' perspective.

Informed by a thorough understanding of how language develops, we should keenly observe what babies are actually doing and how they are responding to the spaces we create, in order to plan appropriate, flexible environments that stimulate speaking and listening skills and reflect babies' individual preferences.

Twelve ideas to try

Inspired by informed practice, we have captured twelve 'places to talk' that reflect the five environmental factors. Each idea is spread over a few pages:

- There is a 'starter' photograph of the space and a description of how it was created.

- We have included some key points about why practitioners selected the materials and resources used.

- There are photographs of children and practitioners using the space, with their comments and some observations of what happened there.

- We have included some action points for you to consider.

You'll see that what we are suggesting doesn't have to cost a fortune. In fact you may already have some of the materials and resources that we have used. What it does involve though, is an informed view and keen observation skills which impact on planning, so that you create the sort of environment that reflects what you want to facilitate for the babies in your setting.

Whilst acknowledging that opportunities for speaking and listening are everywhere, we hope that these ideas will inspire you to review and develop some special 'places for babies to talk' in your environment.

Willow nests

HOW AND WHY?

In this setting, these unusual woven willow spaces were located outdoors because the practitioners wanted to ensure that the outdoor environment was appropriate for the babies they cared for. The spaces were created to encourage babies and adults to enjoy and investigate the outdoor environment and the benefits that brings. Natural light and fresh air support healthy development and the many exciting natural resources stimulate and foster babies' natural curiosity and promote early learning experiences.

The spaces were designed with babies who were not yet fully mobile in mind, as well as those who practitioners had identified as needing a sense of security and containment in a large outdoor space which might be used by other children in a more active way. Physical containment can help to provide the sense of emotional containment which is so important to a baby's well-being. The observed need of many babies to have a safe place to watch from was also key in deciding to create these spaces as well as the use of innately interesting materials. Investigating natural materials offers interest and multi-sensory stimulation for babies which promotes early brain development.

Both spaces were created inexpensively for under £200 by a local craftsman and were made using hazel and willow from sustainable sources. The whole process of construction was documented in pictures to create a further point of interest. Two spaces were created, one small enough for an individual baby and one larger space which could accommodate an adult and a baby together or more than one baby. The willow provided a beautifully textured and naturally multi-coloured surface to investigate and the sides of the nests were made low enough to enable more mobile babies to clamber in and out of the space. The nests were permanently secured to the ground so they couldn't tilt or slip. The spaces were sometimes softened with small cushions and fleeces to add cosiness and comfort.

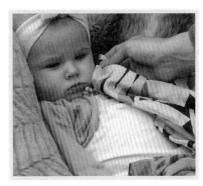

ACTION

What provision do you make for babies in your outdoor space to enable them to confidently investigate and to watch from?

How could you create simple, contained spaces outdoors for babies in your setting?

What might adults have to consider in order to ensure the spaces are truly accessible to babies?

FOR BABIES

Every day routines

HOW AND WHY?

Every day routines are of course necessary aspects of caring for babies, but they are also extremely valuable times for meaningful interaction between babies and their significant adults. As responsive adults nurture and respond to babies, the foundations of social, emotional and language development are formed. However, it is difficult for these interactions to take place if the environment is noisy, busy or uncomfortable. In settings where routines have been thought about from the child's perspective, environments have been created which enable adults to maximise the potential of these everyday routines, turning them into meaningful and pleasurable experiences which promote a baby's sense of being valued, safe and cared for.

Nappy changing is a perfect time for the adult to engage with the baby in dialogue which reflects the shared experience. Jasper is clearly enjoying a dialogue with his mum in a comfortable, uncluttered space which has been created to facilitate this close interaction.

Feeding is a natural opportunity to foster and promote early communication. We can again see Jasper and his mum enjoying a relaxed feeding time in a calm and comfortable space where Jasper is not distracted by his sisters playing close by. This kind of space would be equally appropriate and easy to create in a setting where parents are actively involved in groups and activities. For older babies, meal times can provide the perfect opportunity to be independent and to interact with and learn from peers. In this nursery, babies and older children enjoy their meals together in small groups, sensitively supported by adults who have organised the environment to make it feel homely and to encourage interaction.

The valuable interaction between adult and child at sleeping and waking times is also enhanced by creating a peaceful environment where a key adult can help a baby to fall asleep or to wake up according to their individual needs and preferences. This nursery created peaceful areas both indoors and outdoors where babies can sleep undisturbed either in cots or buggies, where they can easily be observed and where they can have the opportunity to wake in their own time.

ACTION

Observe the routines for babies which take place in your setting – are the places where routines happen comfortable for babies and adults?

How could the environment for routines be enhanced to promote babies' interactions with adults and with peers?

Could the timing of routines be more in tune with babies' individual needs and preferences?

FOR BABIES

Enclosure

HOW AND WHY?

You have probably observed babies, once they become mobile, seeking out enclosed, semi-private spaces such as under chairs, behind curtains or in between units. It's natural for some babies to seek out smaller, enclosed spaces because large spaces can often feel overwhelming for them. You might have experienced babies clinging to your legs in a big, new environment! Smaller spaces feel safer and give a sense of control over the environment. You may also have noticed many babies being attracted to 'softness' within the environment, such as a large soft toy or the cushions on the sofa. This feeling of comfort, together with the more intimate, calmer space, gives babies a place to withdraw to where they can simply sit and watch or process experiences – something babies (and adults!) need time to do in order to make sense of the world and therefore promoting their cognitive, emotional and language development.

Freya was particularly attracted to the enclosed space which had been created at her nursery. It was simply put together using a small 'pop-up' structure with mesh walls which enabled babies to see out of the space. The structure was positioned to make it easily accessible for crawling babies, but was located in a quieter corner of the room, near the window and away from the main flow of movement. A furry rug, large cushions and a soft toy offered appealing textures to explore and material streamers, attached from the roof inside, created interest.

Freya was confident and happy to fall asleep in this cosy space. Because of the mesh walls and open front, it was easy for adults to observe Freya sleeping in her preferred space.

As Freya stirred from sleep, her key worker was able to communicate gently with her from outside her sleeping place, enabling Freya to maintain control of the space and thus the pace at which she re-connected with the world around her.

FOR BABIES

When she was ready, Freya confidently left the space to explore elsewhere. Babies are often sensitive and can be easily overwhelmed when waking from a nap or when they are deeply involved in play, so thinking about the environment we provide can help us to tune into babies' communication and support them at these key times without imposing ourselves on their personal space.

ACTION

Look at your environment from the babies' viewpoint. Are there places which offer enclosure and a sense of privacy which babies can choose to access and to make decisions about what goes on in the space?

How might these spaces alter the interactions you could have with babies?

A PLACE TO TALK

A light and dark space

HOW AND WHY?

In this nursery setting, a space was created which provided a calm, quiet but interesting space big enough for an adult and a baby to explore together. The presence of an interested, emotionally available adult is critical to helping babies to explore their world and to develop their communication skills. The space was positioned at the side of the room on a comfortable rug and was easily created by draping a throw over an existing piece of furniture, which had the effect of slightly darkening the space, making it feel peaceful and cosy. The practitioners had observed that babies were often fascinated with twinkling lights and mirrors, so both were incorporated into the space to provoke interest and exploration.

FOR BABIES

Jamie's key worker, Mahala, gently introduced him to this new environment, enabling him to experience it initially from the safety of her arms. As Jamie became interested in the space, Mahala placed him on his back where he could turn his head to explore. Mahala stayed close to Jamie to provide security and to share the experience with him. Mahala noticed that Jamie was fascinated by the lights and showed that she, too, was interested by looking at the lights and talking about them to Jamie, enabling him to experience her joy in the joint exploration.

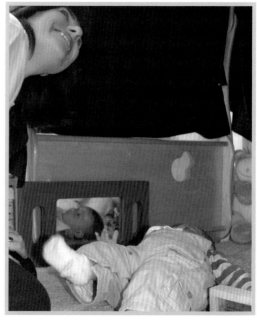

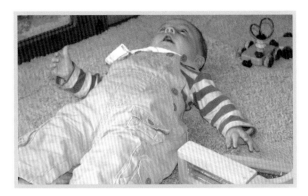

In the pictures we can see Jamie's gaze fixed on the lights and his whole body moving in response to this new experience. Jamie started to vocalise his enjoyment and interest which Mahala responded to, following Jamie's lead in the 'conversation'. The space created the possibility for an extremely valuable and extended interaction between baby, adult and environment. Later, Jamie was joined by his older brother Peter and, supported by their key workers, they were able to enjoy the space in their own way whilst in each other's company, thus fostering important family ties and contributing to each child's sense of self.

ACTION

Where do adults position themselves when interacting with babies in your setting?

Are there places which are comfortable for the baby and the adult to explore together?

Do adults follow the baby's lead as they explore or do they tend to direct the baby's attention?

FOR BABIES

Outside spaces for babies

HOW AND WHY?

Outside spaces are often organised with toddlers and older children in mind, making them less accessible to babies and perhaps less appealing to adults looking after babies who may have concerns over safety. However, outdoors is the perfect place to create a developmentally appropriate environment where babies can experience challenge, risk, excitement and interest, supporting not only their physical development but also their thinking, communication and their sense of self.

These photos demonstrate great use of part of a nursery's outdoor space to create a dedicated baby garden which enables babies to have freedom to explore and play outdoors and which enables adults to have the confidence to support the babies' curiosity and developing independence. In a small, enclosed area, the grass was left to grow to baby height, creating a wild garden which babies could crawl into. From the adult perspective this area seems very ordinary, but looking at it from the babies' viewpoint shows what an intriguing place it is for exploration. Another small area was created for digging, something which many babies enjoy as much as older children. Baby height flower beds and containers were grouped where babies and adults could enjoy, as well as talk about, the shared experience of planting and caring for flowers, fruit and vegetables.

An under-used corner was turned into a screened space for exploring musical instruments by draping fabric over a wooden structure and adding cushions for comfort. This small, appealing space, equipped with developmentally appropriate resources proved to be perfect for mobile babies to gather in and to explore together, but would also be a perfect space for an adult to support a younger baby to explore in the outdoor environment.

To promote physical development, an area was created with wooden planks where babies could independently and safely explore climbing and balancing without having to rely on adults to support them. Of course the thinking involved in exploring this area greatly supported brain development too!

ACTION

How much access do babies in your setting get to the outdoor environment?

What do adults in your setting think about giving babies easy access to the outdoor space?

Do babies have the opportunity to make choices about where to go outdoors and what to do there?

FOR BABIES

Family tins!

HOW AND WHY?

Working in partnership with families is essential to fully understand babies' individual needs, personal preferences and interests, enabling practitioners to 'tune-in' to each baby and to sensitively support their learning and development. It is now well known that when settings take care to create a respectful two-way relationship with parents and to take account of individual family cultures, babies' well-being and development are enhanced. This is especially important when a baby and his/her family are experiencing transition to a new setting. Having meaningful connections with home and family supports the child's sense of security, their developing independence and their overall emotional well-being.

It's important to find ways to facilitate partnerships which families will feel comfortable and motivated to engage with. This setting set up an innovative, low cost, home link project which involved giving each family a large (recycled) tin with a lid, together with some simple guidance about what it was for. Families were asked to use the tins to send images to the setting representing the people and places that their child was most interested in. When the tins were returned, every family had personalised them in their own way, adding to the sense that each family had a special and unique identity. Families said it was useful for them to consider who and what was important and interesting to their child.

One family included pictures of the washing machine, a clock and the microwave as they had noticed that their child was fascinated by them all. This prompted a discussion between the nursery and the family, enabling them both to think about and support the baby's emerging rotational schema.

The personal tins were placed either in a basket or a low table so babies could easily access them and transport the tins and their precious contents indoors or outdoors to be enjoyed and perhaps shared with a significant adult, offering a perfect opportunity for talking and listening.

In the baby room of a setting in Ohio, USA a similar idea was used where photographs of the baby and their family were laminated and placed on low tables. The practitioners realised how very significant these were when they consistently observed babies kissing their own family photos.

ACTION

How can babies in your setting communicate with you about the people, places and objects which are important to them?

Do the ways you currently communicate with families facilitate meaningful two-way communication?

Could you use the environment to strengthen babies' sense of connection to their family while they are in your care?

FOR BABIES

Developmentally appropriate resources for babies

HOW AND WHY?

The resources we provide for babies are a critical part of the environment which we create for them to support and enhance their development. Offering a varied, interesting and developmentally appropriate selection of natural and everyday objects will provoke exploration and imagination and provide the all important sensory stimulation which is essential for babies' brains to develop. Manipulating appropriate resources promotes fine and gross motor skills and concentration and as babies reach to grasp an interesting item, they are learning how to balance and co-ordinate their movements. Resources also make links with the baby's home and family, creating security and placing value on a baby's family culture.

Resources for babies need to be the right size and in the right place for them to access freely with their hands, feet and mouths. The quality of resources is important too, not only to be safe and durable, but also to convey a sense of care and consideration. Because we want to offer choice, it can be a temptation to offer babies too many resources at once which can be very overwhelming for them. A small selection of simple but intriguing resources which can be explored in comfort will often engage a baby for an extraordinary amount of time. The adult role is very important in supporting exploration of resources – showing we are interested in something will naturally create interest from the baby.

Jasper, supported by his mum, is exploring a small selection of stones which have been placed on the floor. Jasper is using his whole body to explore from a sitting position and also whilst on his tummy where he is stretching to reach a stone which has caught his attention. Being on his tummy will help him to develop coordination, balance and postural control which are the foundation for all movement skills including crawling and walking. Tummy time increases babies' independence and confidence to explore their surroundings as they learn to control their bodies.

In this nursery setting, babies are helped to explore interesting resources in the company of an attentive adult. Simple items such as curtain rings placed on a wooden plate, driftwood, a beautiful shell and shredded paper all create interest and excitement and the opportunity to talk about a shared experience.

FOR BABIES

A selection of recycled cardboard tubes in the garden proved to be fascinating for Zach who discovered that the tubes would fall over when he pushed them.

Great thought was given by practitioners to offering resources which enabled this kind of discovery. A simple tray with water and small ducks had the added feature that one duck was a different colour, provoking inquisitive thought and supporting the ability to notice differences.

ACTION

Explore the resources you provide for babies in your setting using your senses, your hands and feet - do these resources provide interest and sensory stimulation?

Are interesting natural and everyday objects always available for babies to explore both indoors and outdoors?

How do practitioners feel about offering babies non-bought resources?

Re-using a travel cot!

HOW AND WHY?

Creating a communication friendly environment for babies can be easily and inexpensively achieved by re-organising and enhancing the existing environment to create places which babies will be drawn to where they can gather, play or watch from. Using careful observation of the places babies prefer to be in as a starting point will help you to decide the kinds of spaces which you could create to support communication and learning. Existing equipment and other resources can often be used in new and unusual ways to create communication friendly spaces.

This nursery setting has a large outdoor area which babies have continuous access to. The practitioners wanted to create a smaller, screened and semi-private space on the large deck area. They used a travel cot, turned on its side, and placed the mattress from the cot on the floor in front which formed an entrance, creating an 'invitation' into the space and a soft place to crawl in or to sit and watch from. Soft, light-coloured cushions were placed inside and a small pale blue camouflage net was draped over the cot – the colours of the resources chosen created a calm space and the mesh sides of the cot which were still partly exposed allowed babies to see out and adults to see in.

Some babies were interested in accessing the space independently, but others were keener to explore and use the space in the presence of a significant adult.

This adult not only provided the feeling of security which some babies needed to give them the confidence to investigate the new space, but also created a natural opportunity to communicate and enjoy each other's company.

As the babies became familiar with the space they really enjoyed being 'tightly packed' in together!

Practitioners also noticed that some babies were more attracted to the space when they removed the camouflage net and spent time exploring the mesh sides and the view through it as well as having conversations with babies on the outside of the space. In order for the environment we create to be truly enabling and accessible, it is important to be flexible and to adapt spaces according to babies' individual needs and preferences rather than hanging on to the adult view of how the space should look.

ACTION

Are there any areas in your setting which babies aren't attracted to or which you don't currently use?

How could you re-organise your existing environment, perhaps using equipment differently, to create spaces which babies will be attracted to?

Consider what your role needs to be to enable babies to investigate and play in the space.

FOR BABIES

Trajectory schema

HOW AND WHY?

Babies, in the same way as toddlers and older children, are fascinated by repeating particular actions over and over again. When we observe babies closely we can often identify patterns, or schemas, emerging. These show us babies' current fascinations which they are drawn to investigate. By offering an environment where babies can explore and extend their schematic play, we are facilitating healthy brain development as the repeated experience facilitates the creation and strengthening of new neural pathways.

In this setting the practitioners noticed that several of the babies were currently fascinated by 'trajectory' and 'going through'. They wanted to introduce new resources which would extend babies' schematic play and exploration.

The practitioners created this simple but effective resource from a piece of drain pipe attached to a memo board with pipe brackets. The cut edge of the pipe was protected with strong tape. Babies were immediately drawn to this interesting new contraption! Some needed support to explore it and enjoyed this joint investigation with an attentive adult. Others let their imaginations run wild, putting all manner of objects in at the top and watching them emerge at the bottom. The brackets were fitted loosely enough around the pipe to enable the position to be changed and some of the older babies noticed that when they moved the pipe round, the items came out in a different direction. Sometimes the practitioners moved the pipe up a little to create a degree of difficulty both cognitively

and physically to further extend the play. The stretching needed to reach the top of the pipe fostered balance and co-ordination skills whilst the 'struggle' needed to insert items was rewarded with a sense of achievement.

ACTION

Over a few days, observe babies in your setting when they are deeply involved in play (using video is a good way to do this). What schemas can you spot?

What spaces could you create and what resources could you use to support and extend the schematic play you have observed?

How could you share your thinking and babies' achievements with parents/carers?

FOR BABIES

Water play

HOW AND WHY?

Exploring the natural world around them is what babies are 'programmed' to do but it's up to us, as adults, to ensure the environment provides the opportunities to do this. Experiencing and investigating water is endlessly fascinating and great fun for babies, enabling them to learn, to think and to communicate their interest and excitement. Outdoors is the perfect location for exploring water where there is no problem with it being transported, poured or spilled as babies find out about and enjoy all the things that water can do.

The photos from this nursery show how water play, offered on the right scale for babies, provides a rich and varied learning environment for young scientists! The water play area was created by setting short, baby-height wooden posts of varying lengths, with plastic guttering attached to the tops, into a concrete base so that water could flow down from one end to the other.

The base created 'hard standing' and was embellished by setting stones into the concrete in a pattern. A bucket of water and some plastic cups were placed nearby and babies were given as much time as they needed to freely explore this outdoor water space.

Practitioners joined the children, encouraging investigation and engagement and talking to the babies about the experience, but did not direct the play, thus supporting independent thought and confidence to try out ideas. The babies enjoyed filling the cups, pouring, watching the water run, using their hands and feet to explore and play as well as having a drink! The babies were able to transport different resources to this area as they followed their individual lines of investigation and developed their ideas in the company of other babies.

ACTION

Do babies in your setting have opportunities to experience and learn about water on an appropriate and accessible scale?

Have you explored water alongside babies lately?

Consider if adults are inhibiting babies' exploration of the world because of concerns around risk or about babies getting dirty or wet.

How could you create a developmentally appropriate space outdoors for babies to freely explore water?

FOR BABIES

Snails

HOW AND WHY?

Having novel experiences and being introduced to something fascinating helps babies to develop confidence and the interest to explore new things. This fosters the courage and motivation needed to overcome difficulties and fears which will benefit babies now and as they grow. The kinds of experiences which older children are excited by could easily be overwhelming or frightening for babies, so getting the scale right when introducing these experiences is crucial but can also be very simple – very many things which adults take for granted are new and different to a baby!

These giant African snails were a new experience for Kitty who, as you can see, is deeply involved in investigation in a small space which was created away from the main flow of movement and where babies could explore these living creatures in a calm and unhurried way. The floor was covered with a small tarpaulin and a piece of carpet was added for comfort. The snails, together with their tanks, were placed on the floor and one snail was placed on some earth in a shallow dish, together with fruit for it to eat.

A small selection of related resources including magnifiers and images were also offered in the space. Using this living resource not only provided an exciting experience but also provided an opportunity for practitioners to foster a sense of care and consideration for other living things by talking to Kitty about how to handle and feed the snails.

This space provided a wonderful tactile experience as Kitty investigated the soil, the fruit and the snails! Putting the tanks on the floor meant they were at baby kneeling height, so Kitty had the opportunity to use all her senses to investigate, not just her sight. The presence of a significant adult supported Kitty but the open-ended nature of the space and the resources meant she could focus on the things which attracted her, helping her even at this young age, to engage deeply for a protracted period of time.

ACTION

Observe babies in your setting investigating new resources – do the resources enable babies to sustain their focus and engagement or are they ignored or quickly discarded?

Think about the kinds of unusual resources you could introduce to the babies you work with and where and how you might offer them. Consider what your role is when introducing babies to a new resource.

FOR BABIES

A sand area inside

HOW AND WHY?

Sand is a brilliant resource which many babies enjoy exploring, but often when sand is provided indoors babies are only able to use their hands to investigate. However, babies like to explore not only with their hands, but also with their whole body. Sand has so many more possibilities (especially for younger babies who cannot yet manipulate implements) if it actually becomes the environment itself, giving babies space to crawl, sit, stretch out and explore.

With these things in mind, this nursery created a large and interesting indoor space which was completely filled with sand. Existing furniture with perspex panels was used to form a boundary to the area, but babies could access it freely. It was big enough for a number of babies to use at the same time even if they all wanted to explore in different ways. The space was not over-cluttered with the kind of toys which might normally be used with sand, but was equipped with a manageable selection of both natural and everyday items. Stones, shells and driftwood were arranged in the sand for crawling babies to access and a wooden 'treasure box' which was accessible to walking babies contained a small number of resources such as buckets, spades and baskets. The way the resources were offered meant that both younger and older babies could easily see and self-select the things they were attracted to rather than having to rely on an adult to help them.

In this exciting indoor space, the babies' attention and interest was focused as they became deeply involved in exploratory play. It is when babies are enabled to sustain their focus in this way that their brains are functioning at the highest cognitive level, promoting thinking and reasoning. In this nursery children play in family groups, so this space enabled children of different ages, including siblings, to interact and learn from one another. Playing and learning together not only introduces younger children to new experiences but also reinforces the learning of older children as they share their ideas and achievements.

ACTION

Could you offer spaces in your setting where resources such as sand could be offered in different ways?

How often do babies get the opportunity to self-select resources in different areas of your setting?

Are there times when babies and older children are able to share experiences and learn together?

FOR BABIES

Action points

Here is a summary of some the questions we posed to prompt action. Use them to reflect on the environment that you currently provide for babies and then to help you focus on making positive changes.

If you look around your environment, what resources and images give status to things that are important and familiar to babies?

Does the way in which you currently communicate with families facilitate a meaningful two-way communication which identifies babies' needs, preferences and achievements?

Are you clear about how best to promote babies' brain development and to support early communication and emotional well-being?

Have you walked around your environment and taken photos recently, especially from the babies' perspective? Is there any unnecessary clutter or areas where babies cannot always access materials due to resource overload?

Do the resources you offer to babies provide sensory stimulation and sustain their focus and engagement and are babies able to access resources independently?

Do the spaces and the resources you provide for babies enable them to follow and develop their current fascinations and emerging schemas?

Do adults enable babies to freely and confidently investigate and play, according to their individual preferences, or are adults sometimes over-directive?

Do you make the most of your outside area to offer babies rich opportunities to investigate, observe, listen and interact with other children and adults?

Do babies have access to quieter, comfortable, inviting areas which are the right size just for one baby or for a baby and an adult to enjoy time together?

Look around your environment – where are the unused corners, equipment and resources that could be used to create cosy, interesting spaces and points of interest to provoke babies' interest and imagination.

Do routines with babies offer opportunities for supporting emotional well-being and developing language in line with babies' individual needs and preferences?

Does your environment offer developmentally appropriate places for babies and young children to spend time and explore resources together?

Useful resources

The resources used to create these 'places to talk' were easy to source, often inexpensive and enhanced existing provision.

Some of the items included:

- Cushions, soft fleeces, scarves and textured woven baskets

- Pop up tents

- Drapes to create darker areas

- Home-made light mobiles

- Soft, textured rugs

- Plants and herbs

- Natural resources like stones and sand

- Recycled cardboard tubing

- Camouflage netting

- Fixings e.g. clamps, pegs, ball ties

- Sand and natural materials

Further references and useful websites

The Communication Friendly Spaces™ Approach Toolkit 2009, Elizabeth Jarman
www.elizabethjarmantraining.co.uk

The Social Baby 2000, Lynne Murray & Liz Andrews, Richmond, Surrey:
CP Publishing

How Babies Think 2001, Alison Gopnik, Andrew Meltzoff & Patricia Kuhl,
London: Phoenix

Rethinking the Brain 1997, Rima Shore, New York: Families and Work Institute

People Under Three 1994, Elinor Goldschmied & Sonia Jackson, London: Routledge

Working with Babies and Children from birth to three 2008, Cathy Nutbrown and
Jools Page, London: Sage Publications

Center on the Developing Child – Harvard University
http://developingchild.harvard.edu/topics/science_of_early_childhood/
particularly: Experiences Build Brain Architecture

Zero to Three - Early Childhood Mental Health
http://www.zerotothree.org/child-development/early-childhood-mental-health/

FOR BABIES

About the author

Elizabeth Jarman is a leading Early Years professional specialising in creating really effective learning environments. She is the founder and managing director of the ELIZABETH JARMAN® Group. Her company is the sole provider of the Communication Friendly Spaces™ Approach which supports communication skills, emotional well-being and increased levels of engaged learning for children across all key stages. Elizabeth's work is widely recognised and respected. Her thinking is professionally challenging the way that environments for children are viewed.

Elizabeth has a background in teaching and worked as an Assistant Director for the Basic Skills Agency, UK where she led national programmes on behalf of the Department for Education.

In Europe, Elizabeth has experience working as lead UK consultant with UNESCO advising on the development of Family Learning schemes. She is currently overseeing a project in Malta on home contexts environments. In the USA, Elizabeth is currently leading an action research project working with Early Intervention Centers in Ohio.

Working with architects to educators, Elizabeth leads an international team of experts who deliver training, deliver consultancy, develop resources and commission research on improving learning environments. She has a particular interest in engaging families in children's learning. Elizabeth writes for the education sector press and has published a number of books on Communication Friendly Spaces™.

Thanks to all of the schools, parents/carers and practitioners who informed and inspired this publication, especially:

A J Crafts, Kent, UK
Norland Nursery, Bath, UK
Red Roofs Day Nursery, Southampton, UK
Townsend Children's Centre, Bournemouth, UK
Strawberry Patch Day Nursery, Norfolk, UK
Hillyer Early Care Pre-school, Ohio, USA
Giggles Day Nursery, Bournemouth, UK
Anne Gladstone, ELIZABETH JARMAN®, UK